For Your Garden

COTTAGE GARDENS

≈ *For Your Garden* ≈

COTTAGE GARDENS

TERI DUNN

FRIEDMAN/FAIRFAX
PUBLISHERS

Dedication

For Lynette Gaslin, queen of sweet peas!

Also for Elizabeth Altman, who has cheered on my writing career ever since Oneonta;
for Larry Maxcy, for the Winston Churchill quote and steadfast encouragement; for
Rachel Strutt, for the love of art and gardens.

A FRIEDMAN/FAIRFAX BOOK

© 1999 by Michael Friedman Publishing Group, Inc.

Library of Congress Cataloging-in-Publication Data available upon request

ISBN 1-56799-784-8

Editor: Susan Lauzau
Art Director: Jeff Batzli
Layout Designer: Meredith Miller
Photography Editor: Valerie E. Kennedy
Production Manager: Richela Fabian

Color separations by Fine Arts Repro House Co., Ltd.
Printed in Hong Kong by Midas Printing, Ltd.

1 3 5 7 9 10 8 6 4 2

For bulk purchases and special sales, please contact:
Friedman/Fairfax Publishers
Attention: Sales Department
15 West 26th Street
New York, NY 10010
212/685-6610   FAX 212/685-1307

Visit our website:
http://www.metrobooks.com

Table of Contents

INTRODUCTION

Trends come and go in the world of garden design, but plants keep on doing what they will. Too much time spent poring over the pages of glossy books and magazines that parade highly manicured landscapes, or too many hours spent gaping at grand gardens that permit tours may blind us to the simple reality that plants just love to grow. This very quality may account for the enduring, homespun popularity of what is sometimes called the "cottage garden."

Just what is a cottage garden? Do you have to have a cottage? The answer to the second question is no, of course not. The answer to the first is a bit more loose. Generally speaking, a cottage garden is a smallish space that is not "designed." Plants are well tended, but they are also allowed to express their natural exuberance. If the sweet peas smother the fence, so be it; if the old-fashioned rose swoons over the herb bed, no matter; if the foxgloves self-sow all over the yard, nobody yanks them out. The cottage garden is informal, lacking in regimentation, allowed to evolve, not overly fussed over. It combines whatever the gardener likes and whatever works in his or her climate or garden situation—perennials, annuals, vines, shrubs, herbs, and roses are all welcome in the cottage plot. The result is a delightful garden that looks a bit overgrown. Lush. Generous. As the British garden writer Mirabel Osler has it, the cottage garden exudes "a gentle chaos."

Such a garden doesn't just happen, however. The most enchanting ones involve thoughtful choices by the gardener. Cheerful color, achieved through a rich mixture of different types of flowers and a healthy dose of green foliage, is one of the hallmarks of the cottage garden. Scent, too, is a basic component of these spaces, and many of the traditional cottage flowers are heavily fragrant.

Certain design elements or accents contribute to the overall feel and success of the garden. You may, for instance, wish to mimic the cottage garden's British origins by making the embracing boundaries pretty with plants (vines, trellises, hedges, and so on). If your yard seems too big for the intimacy you want to evoke, create several garden "rooms." Then fill each space with pretty, easygoing flowers and embellish with atmospheric objects such as attractive containers, statuary, birdhouses, even wind chimes. Cultivate charm. And, most of all, enjoy your garden.

OPPOSITE: With a little research and plant-hunting, you can give an entire bed or area over to one color, and admire the tapestry that develops. Here the theme is predominantly yellow, creating a beam of cheer all the way up to the house. Signature plants in this garden include sneezeweed (*Helenium* spp.), lupines (*Lupinus* spp.), and the deep pink *Filipendula rubra* 'Venusta'.

ABOVE: Poppies, phlox, evening primroses, and many other sweet bloomers crowd a corner near a pergola. Judiciously placed plant supports allow you to get the best use of space out of each plant, and perhaps let you tuck in a few more.

ABOVE: Variety is the soul of the cottage garden, and this vibrant space is alive with an array of colors, textures, and forms. Mixing together an abundance of cottage flowers, such as the drifts of phlox and rose campion (*Lychnis coronaria*) in the foreground, gives you the feeling of lushness that is the key to achieving this style.

OPPOSITE: Spiky perennials seem right at home in each other's company and are a good choice for defined areas such as this pondside bed because they stay within their bounds. The luxuriant bed that encircles part of the pond stands in contrast to the expanse of grass that borders its balance. A classic garden bench is positioned to take advantage of the scene.

ABOVE LEFT: Flowering herbs such as borage (*Borago officinalis*) are just right for cottage gardens. Cottagers once used this plant medicinally to induce a cheerful mood; its modern appeal lies in its modest profile (about two or three feet [60 or 90 cm] wide and tall) and blue or purple star-shaped flowers set against sage green foliage. Grow it among other pastel-hued flowers.

ABOVE RIGHT: Who can resist the nostalgic beauty of sweet peas? They're easy to grow, they come in a wide range of pretty colors and bicolors, and, ah, that heady, orange-blossom fragrance! Pictured here is an heirloom variety called 'Cupani', named for the Italian monk who, long ago, discovered wild sweet peas in the fields of Sicily.

OPPOSITE: Every aspect of a cottage garden ought to be devoted to plants. Here, an abundant-flowering pink climbing rose arches and drapes over the garden gate, creating an impression of profusion even before you enter.

ABOVE: Start the season with early-blooming English wallflowers (*Erysimum cheiri*), cherished not only for their deep, vivid colors, but also for their free-flowering habit and stirring scent. Note that these cottage favorites need well-drained, somewhat alkaline soil in order to perform their best.

OPPOSITE: Believe it or not, every plant you see in this glorious corner "garden" is growing in a pot. Container gardening is a good way to assure a flower-filled stage, because you can always turn, shift, or remove pots to show everything off to its best advantage and to create the full look you want.

BELOW: Closely planted perennials banish weeds and form a beautiful carpet of colors, textures, and forms. The mounding plant in the foreground is a deservedly popular magenta cranesbill, *Geranium sanguineum*. It is prized by cottage gardeners because it is a robust plant that blooms heavily, even in full sun.

ABOVE: A riot of color spills from a collection of pots on a small terrace. The trick to achieving such lushness is to choose eager bloomers, like these pansies, salvias, petunias, and geraniums (the yellow is *Sedum acre*, one of the more prolific of its genus). Then, don't neglect watering, and fertilize generously so the flower show never stops.

ABOVE: Instead of being intimidated by glorious English gardens like this one at Hadspen House in Somerset, borrow their ideas. A crushed gravel path is a lovely touch because it is informal and its soft color harmonizes nicely with plants (it may also keep weeds down). Then plant your flowers right up close to the path's borders, so eventually they will encroach on it, furthering the casual, lush look. Scented herbs sited along the path will release their heady fragrances when brushed by visitors to the garden, another excellent reason to encourage plants to flow onto the walkway.

Chapter One

A COTTAGE GARDEN FOR ALL SEASONS

Every season yields its delights to those who relish being outdoors. This opportunity is no less true in a cottage garden, and indeed, four-season charms can easily be planned. Bulb displays and flowering trees can take the stage early in the year, while foolproof long-bloomers fill in gaps over the sultry summer months. Autumn reveals the glories of late bloomers and beautifully colored foliage, and even winter's frosts can become part of a garden picture if you are not so fussy as to cut back your spent perennials, thus leaving their profiles to host a dusting of snow or a casing of silvery ice.

All of the events of the gardening year ought to be cherished. While a garden at its peak is certainly a breathtaking sight, there are countless more subtle celebrations that take place in the garden throughout the year. In fact, the less-busy seasons give you a chance to slow down and savor the way the personalities of your favorite plants change.

A certain disorder prevails in spring and autumn, perhaps, but it is sweet to pause in the tidying chores. Look around the yard and inhale the scents and moods of a time when your cottage garden is not at its peak. Notice how plants emerge from or return to the fertile earth. At the height of winter, icicles ornament trees, grasses, and statuary, and if you've planned well, the underlying structure of the garden shines through—paths and beds are clearer, walls and arbors more visible.

Full summer is a blessed time, when flowers and fruit are luscious and ripe. This is the season to enjoy the sum of your labors. Set out chairs or stroll slowly along the path and take in the beauty of this romantic garden. Perhaps the greatest lesson of the four-season cottage garden is that the gardener might be wise to loosen his or her grip a bit, to plant and then to let go—and let the garden share its natural inclinations and rhythms.

ABOVE: A favorite in Victorian times and enjoying renewed favor these days is the bright and lovely sweet William (*Dianthus barbatus*), more closely related to the equally fragrant carnation than to the perennial phlox it superficially resembles. Sweet William has stiff stems, which may linger over the cold months. Alas, it is not a long-lived plant, and if you succumb to its charms, you'll have to nurture any seedlings that self-sow or replant every few years.

OPPOSITE: Mix and match a variety of shrubs, perennials, and biennials to be sure color is always present and lush. Here, a pink-themed entry garden is swathed in hollyhocks (*Alcea rosea*), roses, and the profuse-flowering bedding plant blueweed (*Echium vulgare*).

ABOVE: One of the hallmarks of a cottage-style garden is continual color. To that end, you ought to grow a few long-bloomers that you know will pump out plenty of flowers all season long, thus bridging occasional gaps or lapses in the rest of the bed. Here, favorites like lilies and scarlet bee balm fit the bill.

OPPOSITE: Late summer's colors are often bright reds and perky yellows, which certainly set the stage for the changes to come in tree and shrub foliage. Soothing green foliage provides pleasing visual transitions between intensely colored patches of flowers.

ABOVE: England's famous Tintinhull garden, in Somerset, is renowned for its garden rooms, which reveal changing "decor." The neatly trimmed hedge "walls" are a constant in all seasons, but the plants within are given license to encroach upon paths, benches, and lawns for a casual, comfortable look.

OPPOSITE: Impatient for lots of color, early, midseason, and late? Grow vivid, easy annuals. Plant liberally, and crowd the flowers together to achieve the casual but opulent look of the cottage garden. This scheme composed mainly of hot colors—red, orange, and brilliant yellow—evokes the bright, sunny days of summer.

ABOVE: All it takes is some gorgeous tulips to make this shady pathside scene come alive in early spring. Observe how the gardener, while planting dozens of bulbs, did not set them out in a regimented line but rather allowed them to wander up the path.

ABOVE: One way to provide year-round constancy in a cottage garden is to install trellises. Early in the year, or while climbing plants are still young, interest and color can be provided by hanging baskets of blooming annuals.

ABOVE: Pink is a favorite cottage garden theme, and a great many plants are available to oblige the plan. If you are plotting a monochromatic scheme, include different shades and tones of the dominant color. This verdant space makes use of pinks in tones from pastel through magenta. Accents of complementary or contrasting colors are also welcome—a spot of yellow or violet enlivens the scene. Don't forget to include a few anchoring shrubs, such as roses or peonies, among the herbaceous perennials—the shrubs will give the area structure both during the height of bloom and at other times.

OPPOSITE: In an adorable vignette that begins in early summer and, with luck and good weather, lasts for many weeks, silvery *Artemisia latifolia* embraces the tiny-flowered pink rose 'The Fairy'. Bigger, bolder roses, even other pink ones, would be unable to effect this intimate scale or long partnership.

ABOVE: Plenty of sunny yellow daffodils, and perhaps some accompanying primroses, are a sure bet for color early in spring, when the garden needs it most. Later, the planter can be given over to summer bloomers, to ensure that a bright spot of color greets visitors as they pass through the august brick gateway.

OPPOSITE: An imaginative blending of flowers and foliage creates a generous, long-lasting display. White and crimson heathers (*Calluna vulgaris* cultivars) hold court with the dramatic striped ornamental grass *Hakonechloa macra* 'Aureola', silvery artemisias, and traditional autumn asters.

ABOVE LEFT: The tangled canes of 'Scarlet Fire' rose gain surprising beauty as snow and ice decorate them and highlight features less obvious in other seasons, like prickles, faded leaves, and small berries. If you want hips, make sure not to deadhead the flowers—you'll be rewarded by scarlet fruits that add interest through autumn and winter.

ABOVE RIGHT: Frost rims mounds of resting perennials and shrubs, creating a scene of austere beauty in winter's pale sunlight. Yet there is color to be appreciated, a palette of dusky hues from olive green to russet to soft gold to silvery gray. It is the variety that, when truly noticed, rewards the hardy visitor.

OPPOSITE: A fussier gardener might have trimmed back the perennials in autumn and missed this haunting scene. Limned in frost, a herbaceous border takes on a somewhat surreal quality.

Chapter Two

FAVORITE COTTAGE PLANTS

*T*he formula for a lovely cottage garden is based on color, and plenty of it. You want to paint with color, creating not only intimate vignettes, but also beds of plenty, with themes or combinations that harmonize.

The revered English landscape designer Gertrude Jekyll was forever reminding gardeners that "merely having plants, or having them planted unassorted in garden spaces, is only like having a box of paints . . . this does not constitute a picture." She is right, of course, but first you do need a palette.

To that end, presented here are just some of the plants often seen adorning beautiful cottage gardens. How you combine them (with the hope of delighting someone like Jekyll) is a matter of personal taste. There's nothing wrong with copying scenes you admire here or elsewhere—or with dreaming up your own innovative pairings. If you can't find the exact plant you want, focus on color instead. For example, substitute a yellow coreopsis (Coreopsis spp.) for yellow marguerite (Anthemis tinctoria). This way, you'll remain faithful to your palette while making the best use of plants that are available and suited to your area.

Just remember that the plants will teach you—they'll teach you what works and what doesn't, which can vary from one season to the next and indeed from one garden to the next. And sometimes, if you are alert and open-minded, the plants will pleasantly surprise you with their own ideas for placement or combinations. This spontaneity is, after all, part of the joy of gardening in the "cottage" style.

ABOVE: Lovely primroses (Primula vulgaris and others) are the darlings of window box and container gardeners because they grow in nice little rosettes, bloom steadily, and emit a delicate perfume that can be savored at close range. They're certainly hardy enough, however, to grow in the ground in most climates, as long as the soil is moist. Slip primroses in where you need dependable color, or plant a sweep in mixed hues.

OPPOSITE: The scalloped leaves and frothy, yellow-green flowers of lady's mantle (Alchemilla mollis) billow onto a broad path. The plant's genus name translates as "little magical one," a nickname probably derived from the herb's traditional medicinal uses. Today, this charming flower is chiefly used to soften the edges of paths and borders.

RIGHT: For practically effortless all-summer color, and plenty of it, snapdragons are hard to beat. And there's always some to spare for bouquets. Perhaps the finest are the modern hybrid Liberty series, which have fabulous, unmuddied colors and especially strong stems.

BELOW: They look a little bit like another annual, the beloved petunia, but painted tongue (*Salpiglossis* spp.) offers a richer, somehow more elegant, range of colors. You can grow flowers in everything from mahogany red to warm, reddish orange to radiant yellow to royal purple; often, the petals are marbled or penciled with contrasting colors. A mixed bed looks like a richly woven tapestry.

OPPOSITE: Long a mainstay of British cottage gardens, pretty, easygoing wallflowers (*Erysimum cheiri*) come in vivid, cheerful colors, including red, yellow, orange, bright pink, and clear white. They're also deliciously fragrant. The only caveat for most North American gardeners is that the flowers are not terribly cold-hardy. But if you are smitten by these lively blooms, there's no reason you can't plant afresh each summer.

ABOVE: Many flowering herbs make fine choices for the cottage garden, thanks to their appealingly casual profiles. Those in the pink to violet range give you ample opportunity to create vast pastel sweeps. Shown here are purple sage (*Salvia officinalis*) in the foreground, French lavender (*Lavandula stoechas*) in the middle ground, and a clump of spiky bistort (*Polygonum bistorta*) in the rear.

BELOW: Pretty moss phlox or moss pink (*Phlox subulata*) is tough, cold-hardy, tolerant of average or sandy soil, and fairly drought-resistant. The plants have a naturally low, clump-forming habit that likes to spill and weave. This tendency makes them perfect for edgings or for use as groundcovers. Here, the sweet blooms grow up among the stepping stones of a meandering path.

ABOVE: Bellflowers (*Campanula* spp.) are favorites of cottage gardeners everywhere, and no wonder. They are easy to grow and their perky stems are always laden with beautiful, bell-shaped blooms. Look for them in shades of white, China blue, soft pink, and lavender. Grow one or several; they're sure to win you over.

RIGHT: Cottage gardeners naturally gravitate to the older rose varieties, such as this stunning pink damask rose. Unlike the modern hybrid teas, these antique roses tend to smother themselves in both foliage and lovely flowers. The flowers are more casual, too, with loads of petals and intoxicating fragrance to match. More pluses: some of the vintage roses endear themselves to gardeners by being much less disease-prone and more cold-hardy than their modern counterparts.

BELOW: You'll love "cottage pinks" (*Dianthus* spp.) for their generous display of pretty little flowers, their spicy fragrance, and their relaxed, open growth habit. They are a cinch to grow in full sun and ordinary soil (preferably neutral or even a bit alkaline). When their exuberant blooming slows down, shear them back and watch for an encore.

OPPOSITE: Just two well-chosen plants create a fabulous scene: the old-fashioned, shrubby 'Rosa Mundi' rose (also called *Rosa gallica versicolor*), with its random pink-and-crimson-splashed petals, consorts with the bold, lime green flower heads of a euphorbia plant.

ABOVE: A thriving large-flowered clematis vine, such as the regal cultivar 'Victoria', is a joy to behold. A few tips for copying such a display: you need to find a spot that offers fun sun (like this fence) but cool shade for the shallow roots; plant the vine in rich, well-drained soil; mulch to retain soil moisture as well as to keep weeds at bay; and water regularly. Be patient, for the vines don't really start flowering heavily until they've been established for a couple years.

ABOVE: Gorgeous stalks of lupines rise above the throng in early summer, announcing "cottage garden" to all who pass by. They do best in areas with cooler, moister summers such as New England, Canada's Maritimes, and the Pacific Northwest.

ABOVE: A little too effusive to be grown by tidy gardeners, four o'clocks (*Mirabilis jalapa*) are sprawling plants that cover themselves in irresistible, trumpet-shaped blooms in tropical shades of red, magenta, fuchsia, yellow, and white, and may even sport stripes. The plant's name refers to the fact that the flowers don't pop open until late afternoon—something to look forward to when you come home from school or work. Four o'clocks are also extremely popular with hummingbirds and evening moths.

RIGHT: A survey of garden catalogs or well-stocked local nurseries will turn up all sorts of enticing columbines, like this gorgeous red and yellow of the McKana Giants strain. Some columbines are large-flowered, some are tiny, some are tall, some are dwarf; they come in mixes; and lovely solid-color varieties provide an alternative to the bicolor schemes. Many of the newer hybrids trace their parentage back to the dainty, original red and yellow wildflower *Aquilegia canadensis.*

OPPOSITE: No cottage garden should be without some hollyhocks (*Alcea rosea*) to greet visitors near a gateway or door, or to lean along a fence or hedge. Though technically biennials—plants that bloom in their second year of growth, then fade—hollyhocks self-sow dependably and produce extras at the base of mature plants, so there are always plenty each season. New double, or powder-puff, varieties are available, but the single-flowered old-fashioned types are the most charming. Shown here is 'Nigra', which is closer to maroon than black.

ABOVE: Exuberant sweet peas (*Lathyrus odoratus*) love to climb, clinging to supports such as fences, trellises, and pillars with their delicate-looking tendrils. They're generous with their ruffled, deliciously scented blossoms, too. If you need to rein in a burgeoning clump, start picking bouquets!

OPPOSITE: There's nothing rare or unusual here, just white petunias and feverfew (the larger, double-flowered kind, most likely *Tanacetum parthenium* 'Plenum'). But all that eager, flourishing white creates a downright exciting picture. All-white gardens are especially charming late in the day, when the flowers seem to glow in the soft light of evening.

BELOW: Early cottagers grew a variety of fruits and herbs in their small plots, so why not include some delicious strawberries in your cottage garden? They're as pretty as they are tasty, and their rich, sun-warmed scent will beckon as they ripen. Tuck them into any well-prepared, fertile bed.

Chapter Three

DEFINING THE BOUNDS

*T*raditional cottages in English villages, or at least in our fantasies, have pretty little white fences around the small yards. Or perhaps they are edged with venerable stone walls, aged with olive green lichens. Arbors or swinging gates greet visitors.

Well, even if you don't garden in such a setting, the idea of defining the garden's bounds is both practical and appealing. Many of us don't have sprawling properties, and an enclosed garden offers refuge and privacy from the neighbors, as well as respite from noise and from the outside world in general. Moreover, defined boundaries provide a sense of what is yours (and what is not). Indeed, the cottage garden ideal is perfectly workable for the modern suburban or urban dweller, and is even possible for the rural gardener who wishes to carve out a small, cultivated haven.

It is important, though, to integrate the boundary markers into your garden. Let no fence or wall go unadorned; instead, plant them with climbing vines or espaliered trees, or allow mixed borders awash with flowers to soften wall surfaces. Fill corners of the patio and front entries with pots of blooms, and line paths, straight or curving, with billowing plants. Hang baskets, erect trellises, interject pillars. Let this thought be your guiding principle: It may be a small world, but it shall be bountiful.

OPPOSITE: If you are lucky to have a stone retaining wall in your cottage garden, by all means plant on, in, and around it, so that it becomes not merely a boundary but a member of the garden. Lavenders, like the vivid 'Munstead' cultivar shown here, are a lovely match because they prefer the light, well-drained soil that often prevails in a wall's vicinity. Plus, the lavender offers the pleasing bonus of fragrance. If you have a dry rock wall (one that lacks mortar), you might also opt to plant a few rock garden favorites in and among the stones of the wall itself.

ABOVE: While you don't wish to crowd a gateway and prevent passage, an abundance of adjacent plants can serve as a warm welcome. The towering *Miscanthus* 'Silver Light' to the left of this gate is an inspired choice, because ornamental grasses retain their beauty in all seasons. The pale pink Japanese anemones in front of the gate don't bloom until late summer or autumn, but they are truly spectacular.

ABOVE: When planning a cottage garden, choose billowing plants at every opportunity. 'New Dawn', an outstanding, everblooming climbing rose, clambers enthusiastically over the fence and gate, while lady's mantle (*Alchemilla mollis*) blankets the sides of the walkway.

OPPOSITE: The scale may be a bit grand, but the scene has some ideas worth borrowing. A see-through gate makes a garden more inviting, particularly if your garden walls or flanking pillars are heavy. And growing sprawling plants just outside the gate softens the entrance (here, the border is planted primarily with easy-to-grow cranesbill geraniums and lady's mantle).

ABOVE: A path, particularly a straight one, has little hope of being inviting until the garden grows up around it—and, in time, perhaps leans a bit over the walkway's rigid line. Once the flowers have filled in, the path leads visitors onward, but the living ornaments along the way slow their steps, encouraging them to savor the journey.

ABOVE: A living wall, such as this thick hedge, will enclose a garden beautifully. The green backdrop can be quite complementary to the profusion of flowers typical in the cottage garden. However, you will have to shear the hedge regularly to encourage it to grow densely and to keep it in bounds and looking tidy. So don't forget to allow for some access along its length.

ABOVE: Areas near high walls will be fairly shady, especially early and late in the day. Moderate the stone wall's impression of solidity by leaving the door open and by inviting plants to grow up and over the enclosure. Devoting the beds in the wall's shade to pale-colored or white flowers will also lighten the space.

OPPOSITE: Brick paths, while durable and handsome, do need some help in acquiring that desirable "lived in" look. Pathside flowers are an obvious idea, but don't forget taller, arching blooms, shrubs, ornamental grasses, towering herbs, even a small ornamental tree or two. If the path is not strictly mortared, a bit of moss or a small, creeping groundcover might also be welcome.

ABOVE: The secret to this garden's overgrown look is close planting of carefree favorites, among them milky bellflower (*Campanula lactiflora*), hollyhocks, and the rambling rose 'American Pillar'. A squared arbor set over the path gives you the opportunity to carry color high into the sky and punctuates the length of the path, creating a sense of mystery about what lies beyond.

ABOVE: When laying a flagstone path, place the broader stones on the terrace or patio, and use the smaller ones as you move further away. People approaching the house will feel welcomed, while those entering the garden will be drawn into the distance. Then grow ample plants or shrubs in the distance to create a sense of fullness, even if your garden is on the small side.

ABOVE: An adobe house in the American Southwest gets the "cottagey" look, thanks to a lush, enveloping garden—and a defining fence. Note how the plain fence echoes the colors of the house's trim, with posts left unfinished to complement the warm color of the adobe. Something more ornate would have called too much attention to itself or clashed with the house. And in keeping with the gardener's goal, roses and other plants are allowed to grow on, over, and around the fence, softening its lines while still letting it do its job.

OPPOSITE: Free-blooming, cream-colored flowers are wonderful companions for an informal stone wall. The rose is 'Iceberg', prized for its heavy, repeat bloom (one spray may contain as many as a dozen lovely roses, so sneak a few for bouquets!). Also in attendance are 'Congratulations' lilies and a white calamint.

ABOVE: If you want loads of color bursting the bounds of your cottage garden, select a self-sower like valerian (*Centranthus ruber*). In cool regions, especially, this perennial plant will carry on all summer. It comes in pink or white.

BELOW: The aptly named 'Blaze' rose covers itself from top to bottom in clusters of blooms. If you are going to use roses in your cottage garden—and you certainly should, for they are classic—you'd do wise to select ones like this favorite, ones that are not fussy and will bloom over a long period.

ABOVE: Fill a corner, disguise a foundation, or enliven an entryway with the fountains of bloom of a shrubby, easygoing rose. Shown here is 'Ballerina', which produces great sprays of small, white-centered pink blooms for the better part of the summer.

Chapter Four

EMBELLISHMENTS

*A*dding decoration to your cottage garden can be great fun. It's not unlike the moment when, after you have moved all the furniture into a new room, you stand in the doorway with pictures, vases, mementos, and statuettes, ready to embellish the scene. Outdoor decor, of course, needs to be durable and weather-resistant, but other than that, there are no limits save your imagination. You certainly also have the same freedom to move items about, to stand back and see how you like the effect, and to make changes later as need or whim dictates.

Embellishments that bring a "cottagey" feel ought to be pretty in their own right, even as they harmonize with the garden. Seek out old pots and containers, or look for new ones that have beautifully ornate detailing. Add a whimsical birdhouse or a charming little birdbath, either of which will also bring the bonus of glorious songbirds to your garden. Items like lampposts, sundials, and found objects are also nice, and may be practical as well as decorative. Search flea markets, tag sales, and antiques shops for garden accents that will bring a homey touch to your cottage plot. Alternatively, shop specialty catalogs and garden centers that carry a selection of accents with old-fashioned appeal.

Remember that all of these decorative objects serve a purpose. They add enriching character to your garden, surely, but they also contribute to the impression of profusion. They'll add to the pleasure and pride you'll feel every time you step out to enjoy your cottage garden.

OPPOSITE: Mixing textures is a great trick for making a small space seem more expansive. Here, an unused doorway becomes a small but complex garden space; the wooden doors, stone wall, terra-cotta pots, and diamond-shaped pavers contribute a wealth of different surfaces and colors. Weaving these textures together is a pleasant selection of plants, among them tall abutilons, geraniums, and browallia.

ABOVE: An old-fashioned water pump emerges from a flower bed. Old, dilapidated ones may no longer function, but will still bring personality to the garden. If you find a pump that works, it may really come in handy, either as a water outlet (for filling watering cans or hooking up a hose) or as the focal point of a small decorative fountain.

ABOVE: Don't have a thatched cottage? No matter. Erect one for the birds, and your garden instantly gains that coveted English mood. Setting the feeder on a pole is not only practical for the birds, this measure also keeps the feeder from being overcome by eager plants.

RIGHT: A bed of lavender goes from staid to elegant with the introduction of a handsome sundial, raised on a pedestal so it stands out. Like the lavender, a sundial is meant to be placed in full sun, so the pairing works on a practical level, too.

OPPOSITE: Glorious clematis and fragrant sweet peas practically smother a charming lamppost in their embrace, a testament to a successful idea. The post provides valuable support for the climbers, while the flowers lend added grace to a classic lighting fixture. The gardener may have to intervene now and then with clippers to make sure the light itself isn't lost from sight.

ABOVE: Window boxes are a great way to add more flowers to your garden. Just be sure that sturdy brackets are supporting the weight and that the box has some allowance for drainage so the plants within can thrive. With well-planned window boxes, even city gardeners and those with a minimum of time for maintenance chores can enjoy a profusion of bright blooms—these are petunias mixed with nicotiana.

ABOVE: A window frame set with panes of mirror reflects the beauty of the garden back on itself. Incorporating mirrors into rooms, a strategy popular with interior decorators, works as well in the garden as in the parlor; just be sure that the mirror reflects an enchanting scene rather than your garden's flaws. Here, a "window box" full of verbena, lobelia, and geraniums offers dependable, summer-long color.

ABOVE: Trees finished blooming? Why not hang some colorful baskets of annuals from the branches. There will be no illusion that these giddy flowers belong to the tree—instead, the impression will be of burgeoning color from all sides of the container.

OPPOSITE: Blur the edges of a patio or terrace with plenty of potted plants. If those out in the garden begin to approach the house, over time, the effect will be that of continuous growth. Keep the show interesting by choosing unorthodox plants for the pots, perhaps ones that are too tender to overwinter in the ground anyway; shown here are dracaena (*Cordyline australis*), *Cerinthe major* 'Purpurascens', diascia, and shrubby, bell-laden fuchsia.

BELOW: This gardener made a point of choosing a range of pots. They are all made of clay, but each one is an individual, as is the plant tucked into it. The result is a full and lively display.

ABOVE: A strawberry jar filled with 'Pink Panda' strawberries sits stoically atop a low garden wall. The lush background of flowers and foliage helps to integrate the large pot into the garden, while the pink flower heads of *Centranthus ruber* look up adoringly. You can certainly use strawberry jars for other plants as well, but first make sure that the intended plants can survive the tight space.

ABOVE: The ball shape of the ornamental allium's purple flowers are echoed by the stout, rounded urn in their midst. Thanks to the urn's commanding size, the entire bed gains extra heft and dimension—this trick works particularly well in small gardens.

ABOVE: The musical tinkle of wind chimes brings a touch of enchantment to any outdoor space. Instead of hanging the chimes from the porch, why not attach them to a tree branch, arbor, or sturdy shrub right out in the garden?

OPPOSITE: An informal, maturing garden is best served by a casual path; note the way that the stones are irregularly shaped and spaced, either deliberately or from years of use. An elegant urn set on a squared pedestal adds greatly to the garden's charm and invites the wandering visitor to pause a moment.

ABOVE: Overflowing window boxes are always desirable, but what makes this scene so charming is the lavish use of color. The bright yellow window frame and blue house are well matched by the variety of bold-hued flowers; a more conservative tack, such as a few yellow flowers, wouldn't create nearly the excitement and beauty of this vignette. Plenty of silvery foliage below the window balances the scene.

ABOVE: Daring color works its magic as crimson, purple, and pink flowers frolic in a bright white planter at the base of a pink wall. You needn't redo your house's paint scheme front and back to achieve such a combination; just try some strategic swathes along a wall or fence.

INDEX

PHOTO CREDITS